TRANSFORMATIVE LEADERSHIP

vulnerability

authenticity

TRANSFORMATIVE

empathy

LEADERSHIP

humility

grace

JOSHUA P. TROUT

PALMETTO
P U B L I S H I N G
Charleston, SC
www.PalmettoPublishing.com

Copyright © 2024 by Joshua P. Trout

All rights reserved

No portion of this book may be reproduced, stored in a retrieval system, or transmitted in any form by any means–electronic, mechanical, photocopy, recording, or other–except for brief quotations in printed reviews, without prior permission of the author.

Paperback ISBN: 979-8-8229-4231-8
eBook ISBN: 979-8-8229-4232-5

Contents

Introduction vii
Chapter 1: Dodging Early Curveballs 1
Chapter 2: Leading Through the Storm 6
Chapter 3: Resilience Unveiled: Shaping a Leader Through Trials 15
Chapter 4: Turning Scars into Leadership Gold 20
Chapter 5: Nurturing Growth and Empowering Others 26
Chapter 6: Riding the Rollercoaster of Success and Setbacks 32
Chapter 7: The Compass of Transformative Leadership and
    Cultivating Your Core Values 37
Chapter 8: My Personal Core Values: Embracing Vulnerability,
    Empathy, Grace, Authenticity, and Humility 43
Chapter 9: Putting It All Together: Transformative Leadership 54
Chapter 10: Passing On the Torch 61
Conclusion 68
Study Workbook 71
Acknowledgements 79
In Loving Memory 83

Introduction

Hey there! Have you heard of West Newton, Pennsylvania? It's a little spot most folks zip past on the map without a second glance, tucked away and cozy with its tight-knit vibes. But you know what? Sometimes the places we grow up in, the spots we call home, kinda shape who we are. For me, West Newton isn't just a place on a map; it's like a symbol for figuring out my smallness in this massive universe.

Throughout this book, I'll take you on a ride through my ups and downs, my wins, and those eye-opening moments when I realized I'm part of something bigger. It wasn't all fairy tales and sunshine during my growing-up years, but it wasn't a total sob fest either. My life's been stitched together with plenty of rough patches, but also some pretty awesome breakthroughs.

Nowadays, I'm out here leading, but once upon a time, I couldn't even picture myself in charge of anything. Life felt like I was just floating along without a clue. But if you're here for a story that'll lift you, and show you how to turn things around, you're in the right spot.

This isn't your typical rags-to-riches or flashy success story. It's about hanging tough, beating the odds, and figuring out that, heck, I was cut out for leading all along. So let's hit the road on this super personal journey from feeling irrelevant to getting inspired, from doubting myself to stepping up as a leader.

Every chapter, and every challenge, has shaped me into who I am today. And what I've learned? It's all applicable to you too. You can rise from tough times and lead. If you're ready, let's get this story started.

Unveiling the Past: From Hesitation to Leading the Charge

As we walk down memory lane, you'll bump into those key moments that spun my life around. Old scars might show up that threw shadows of doubt my way. But in those shaky times, I found some serious inner mojo—that solid determination that pushed me from feeling empty to rocking the top spots.

This journey's been real—no sugarcoating here. It's been rough, with setbacks and hurdles that seemed huge, and yeah, doubt did sneak in sometimes. But every rough patch taught me something and turned into a launch pad for something better.

At the core of it all was this deep-down belief that kept me going through the darkest times and lit up my best days, whispering, "You're meant for big things."

Iron Sharpens Iron: Tough Times Make Tougher People

We've all got that little voice inside pushing us to break past our limits, to shoot for the stars. I'll dive into how to listen to that voice, boost it, and believe in yourself. My story's out in the open here, and I'm hoping it hits home with you.

When life throws curveballs, that's where you grow. Like iron sharpening iron, challenges refine us. They're like a forge for our character, toughening up our resilience. The grind of facing hard stuff isn't just tough—it's what builds us up.

Adversity isn't just a hurdle; it's a stepping-stone that sharpens our minds, strengthens our spirits, and sets us on the path to progress.

Think of tough times not as a curse, but as a tough-love teacher shaping tough-as-nails souls. It's a class for the unstoppable, with lessons that forge unbeatable characters. Let's take these lessons in stride as we explore self-discovery, real-deal vulnerability, and genuine leadership.

As we roll from doubt to leading the pack, I hope my tales light a fire in you to carve your trail—whether that's making it big in the business world or finding your peace and purpose closer to home.

So buckle up—this tale of guts, leadership, and growth is about to unfold, and I hope it speaks to your heart, lighting your way forward. Let's get this journey started, breathing life into these words and chasing new horizons together.

A Tough Start: Battling the Odds

My life wasn't handed to me on a silver platter. It's been about tackling giant hurdles, fighting the odds, and finding my strength from day one.

From early on, I faced health battles that seemed to just keep coming: high fevers, too many hospital rooms, and a whole lot of time feeling cut off from normal kid stuff. It was a rocky start, to say the least.

There were ear problems that had me in and out of surgery from when I was just a little kid. Those setbacks kept me quiet, kinda stuck in my shell during those early years.

But at three years old, I started breaking out of that silence with a program that aimed to get me talking. It was tough, frustrating even for a little kid, but it sparked something in me—a drive to not just sit back and accept things as they were.

School wasn't easy either. Being different made me an easy target, but a throwaway comment from a counselor—that I'd be "lucky to work at McDonald's"—lit a fire under me. Choosing to repeat a grade was my call, a move to prove I wasn't about to let anyone write my story for me.

That fight for respect carried me through, from standing up to those who doubted me to finding my tribe among those who were also left on the fringes. High school was about forging deeper connections and discovering the joy of lifting others.

My purpose came alive when I started volunteering at the fire department during my high school days. It's where I felt part of something bigger, and a dramatic rescue locked in my decision to chase a career in emergency medicine.

Thirteen years on the front lines as a firefighter and EMT taught me resilience like nothing else. But the pull to do more kept tugging at me.

Diving into health care and pursuing further education opened up so many opportunities, but it also came with a lot of doubts. I was constantly questioning whether I was on the right path and whether I could handle the challenges. But everything changed when I met the right mentor at just the right time. He pushed me past my excuses and showed me what I was truly capable of.

If there's one piece of advice I'd give to anyone, it's this: you don't know everything. And that's okay. Finding a mentor is crucial. Work with your mentor, learn from that person's experiences, and soak up as much wisdom as you can. Trust me, it makes all the difference. Let's dive into the whole mentor thing. Trust me, having a mentor can be a game-changer in your life and career. But how do you actually find one? And what should a mentor do? Let's break it down.

Every chapter, and every challenge, has shaped me into who I am today. And what I've learned? It's all applicable to you too. You can rise from tough times and lead. If you're ready, let's get this story started.

CHAPTER 1

Dodging Early Curveballs

*Success is not final, failure is not fatal:
it is the courage to continue that counts.*
—Winston Churchill

Rewind to my earliest days and you'd see a kid described with two tough labels: sick and underprivileged. These weren't just words; they painted the picture of my early life—a tapestry stitched together with chronic illness and money woes. In this chapter, we're diving deep into those early battles, each met head-on with grit, turning tough times into stepping-stones for change.

The story starts with a bit of a shocker—an enlarged spleen, something I didn't even know I'd had until later in life. At three months old, I was already set apart, missing out on those basic cuddles that mean so much between a parent and child. Not being held much left a mark, kind of a shadow that hung around, making me always feel a bit left out, always craving more closeness.

As I grew, new challenges popped up, such as issues with my ears and speaking. You might think these are small bumps on the road of life, but for me, they were huge. Constant trips to doctors, getting ear tubes put in and taken out, and wrestling with speaking and learning problems all cast a long shadow over my young years.

Back then, getting help for learning differences wasn't easy. My folks were in a constant struggle to find support to help me catch up. Easterseals, a lifeline for kids and adults with disabilities, was a beacon of hope amid these tough times. But even with their help, the road was anything but smooth, leaving lasting impressions on my journey.

One memory that stands out is from elementary school, when a counselor casually said I'd be lucky to land a job at McDonald's. That kind of put-down stung, especially coming from someone who was supposed to support me. But it also lit a fire in me, sparking a fierce desire to prove them wrong and push past the barriers that made me different.

It wasn't just about overcoming academic hurdles. My childhood was packed with doctor visits and lots of missed school, adding layers of complexity to already tough times. At home, the vibe was tense, with my parents—especially my mom—always on edge, worried sick about me.

Childhood's supposed to be all about fun and carefree exploration. Not for me. Biking wasn't a breeze down the street; it was a carefully guarded activity right out front, with all the protective gear you can imagine. Those ideal summer days playing with friends were swapped for feeling isolated and dreaming of something more.

Then there's the part about being "disadvantaged." Despite my dad's hard work with long hours and my mom's creative side hustles, money was always tight. Forget fancy trips; just making ends meet was our family's reality. The constant shadow of financial trouble was always there, looming over us.

In all this mess, I made a silent promise to myself—I wouldn't let these tough times define my future. The entrepreneurial spirit I saw in my family inspired me. They were always trying to make something out of nothing, turning every skill into a potential paycheck. This struggle to stretch every dollar taught me more about resilience and determination than anything else.

The Creative Hustle at Home

Growing up, my parents were the epitome of hustle and creativity, always finding unique ways to make ends meet. Our home was a hub of activity and ingenuity, and their entrepreneurial spirits were the lifeblood that kept us going.

My mother was a wizard with her hands. She had a knack for crafts that could transform everyday items into pieces of art. She'd spend hours at the kitchen table, surrounded by colorful fabrics, glitter, and glue, turning out handmade decorations, personalized gifts, and home decor items that she sold at local craft fairs. Her skills didn't stop there, though.

Mom was also a phenomenal baker. Her cookies, cakes, and pies were the stuff of legend in our neighborhood. Every holiday season, our house smelled like a bakery, with trays of cookies lining the countertops. She even ventured into the world of chocolate, opening a small store that sold chocolate and molds for other bakers to make their sweet treats. Watching her juggle these various ventures, I learned the importance of passion and dedication. She showed me that creativity could be a powerful tool to help make ends meet and bring joy to others.

On the other side of the hustle spectrum was my dad. A Navy veteran, he worked multiple jobs post-service to provide for our family. His schedule was grueling—long hours and plenty of overtime. But no matter how tired he was, he never lost his drive to do more.

Dad had a deep-seated entrepreneurial bug. He started an Italian ice cart that he would take to local events, making extra money and bringing smiles to many faces on hot summer days. I remember tagging along with him, eager to help and soak up his enthusiasm. It was during these times that I learned the value of hard work and the importance of seizing opportunities whenever they arose.

One of the most inspiring things about my dad was his relentless pursuit of his dreams. In his forties, when most people might be settling into their routines, he decided to go back to school. He enrolled in the local community college to study culinary arts, fulfilling a long-held dream of becoming a chef.

It wasn't easy balancing school with work and family, but he did it with determination and grit. His perseverance paid off, and soon enough, he graduated and started his own catering company. This venture eventually led to owning his own restaurant, a testament to his belief that it's never too late to chase your dreams.

Dad's journey from Navy vet to chef and entrepreneur wasn't just inspiring—it was delicious. His culinary skills were top-notch, but his cheesecake was the pièce de résistance. Creamy, rich, and perfectly balanced, it became the highlight of many family gatherings and celebrations.

My parents' creative hustles and entrepreneurial spirits shaped my childhood and taught me invaluable lessons. From my mom, I learned that creativity and passion can be powerful tools to make a difference and bring happiness to others. From my dad, I learned the value of hard work, the importance of perseverance, and that it's never too late to chase your dreams.

Their stories are a testament to the power of ingenuity and determination, and they've inspired me to bring the same level of hustle and creativity to my endeavors. Whether it's in my professional life or personal projects, I carry their lessons with me, always striving to honor the spirit of entrepreneurship and hard work they instilled in me.

From Struggle to Strength

Instead of dragging me down, the rough start to my life shaped me and molded my character in ways I couldn't have imagined. I don't hold any grudges against my parents; they did their best in a wild ride of life. I focus on how those tough years prepped me to be who I am now—someone who values compassion and helping others over chasing bucks.

As we move on from the rough patches of my early life, the next chapters will reveal how I transformed those struggles into strengths. This isn't just a story about hard times; it's a salute to human resilience. Every hurdle I faced turned into a step forward, proof of how tough times can lead to great leadership, and a reminder of the unbeatable spirit within us all.

Looking back at my earliest days, it's clear that being labeled as sick and underprivileged wasn't just a description; it was the reality that shaped my life. From dealing with an enlarged spleen at three months old to battling ear issues and learning difficulties, every challenge left a mark. These early struggles were more than bumps in the road—they were mountains that I had to climb.

My journey was filled with doctor visits, missed school, and constant battles for support. When I heard the counselor's discouraging words in elementary school, I became determined to prove him wrong. My home life, marked by financial struggles and my parents' tireless efforts, taught me resilience and the value of hard work.

Watching my parents hustle to make ends meet was a lesson in creativity and perseverance. My mom's craft skills and baking talent, combined with my dad's entrepreneurial ventures, showed me that it's never too late to chase your dreams. Their stories inspired me to bring the same level of hustle and creativity to my own life.

Instead of letting these tough times define me, I chose to let them shape me into a person who values compassion and helping others. The next chapters will delve into how these early struggles were transformed into strengths, highlighting the power of human resilience.

CHAPTER 2

Leading Through the Storm

Every adversity, every failure, every heartache carries with it the seed of an equal or greater benefit.
—Napoleon Hill

Reflecting on my journey, it's clear that it's woven from wins and high fives as well as countless challenges and setbacks that tested my grit. Adversity wasn't just a roadblock; it was like a constant travel buddy through my leadership journey. The real grit of leadership gets hammered out in these tough times, and the lessons I picked up have become the bedrock of how I lead and inspire others.

The Birth of Vulnerable Leadership

In the heat of those tough times, I uncovered the key to what I call 'vulnerable leadership'—a game changer not sparked by a sudden lightbulb moment but shaped over time through my own trials and tough breaks. There were moments when throwing in the towel seemed like a tempting option and the road ahead looked like a dead end. But it's through these moments, little by little, that I began to understand true leadership.

In the darkest times, I had this moment of clarity that rocked my perspective. Giving in to despair wasn't just about me; it felt like turning my back on life itself—a life that's not just mine but also shared with others. I realized we're all threads in this giant tapestry of life, each playing our part, lifting each other up. It's easy to miss how much we can light up someone else's world, offering a spark of hope or inspiration just when it's needed most.

Thinking about quitting made it clear to me that dimming my light would shortchange not just myself but also anyone who might find a little peace or courage from my story. Life's a team sport, and our struggles and victories sing in harmony with others. As I navigated my maze of challenges, I saw that showing my vulnerable side wasn't just about personal growth—it was also a chance to stretch beyond myself and offer something truly valuable to others on similar paths. Vulnerable leadership unfolded for me not in dramatic revelations but in quiet moments of real talk with myself. It's about seeing our rough spots not as flaws to hide but as strengths to embrace. Through our own battles, we can light the way for others fighting their own, offering hope and a path forward.

Leading Through Adversity

As we dive into this chapter on leading amid adversity, we'll look at those crunch times that demanded every ounce of courage, endurance, and belief in a better tomorrow. I'll share those turning points where stumbling blocks turned into launch pads for change and creativity—from navigating unexpected setbacks to tackling what seemed like impossible odds.

We'll explore the deep essence of leadership, woven through with persistence, ingenuity, and a spirit that refuses to back down, pushing us ever forward. Adversity and openness about our vulnerabilities reveal not just what we can do but also our ability to lead with purpose and heart. Let's gear up to take in the full measure of what adversity teaches us and discover the immense power that springs forth when leadership meets life's curveballs head-on.

An Unknown Journey: Firefighter/EMT

It might seem weird that my mom supported my decision to become a firefighter, especially considering how anxious she was during my early years. You can imagine her reaction when I decided to jump into even more danger. But to get why she was okay with it, let's dive into the heart of our tight-knit community.

Growing up, our neighbors were like family, and the volunteer fire department was a big deal in our town. It wasn't just about fighting fires; it was about community, responsibility, and sticking together. Everyone knew everyone, and the fire department was a symbol of our collective spirit and our willingness to help each other out.

When I told my mom I wanted to join, she wasn't thrilled about the danger, but she got it. She knew being a volunteer firefighter wasn't just about the adrenaline or the risks; it was about being there for our neighbors when they needed us most. It was about service, duty, and the bond that held our town together.

So, while it might have seemed like a crazy choice, in our community, it made perfect sense. My mom's support came from understanding what it meant to be part of something bigger than ourselves. It was this sense of community and shared responsibility that defined us, and it's something I carry with me to this day.

In western Pennsylvania, being a volunteer firefighter was as natural as breathing. It was a testament to our tight-knit community and the values we held dear. This experience shaped me in ways that go beyond just the skills I learned; it instilled in me a sense of duty, camaraderie, and a deep appreciation for the power of community.

In our little town, volunteer fire departments were the backbone of our safety. When disaster struck, these were the brave souls who ran straight into danger. Despite my mom's fears, nostalgia ran deep in our family. My grandpa had been a firefighter, and my mom had a strong sentimental attachment to this heritage. So, against all odds, I found myself wearing the uniform of a junior firefighter.

The fire department became my refuge, my purpose, and my escape from judgment. The solidarity was palpable as soon as I walked through the station doors. Those years as a junior firefighter were a time of massive growth and learning for me, and the stories I have from those days could fill volumes. Maybe one day, my friend Mike and I will write down the countless EMS stories we've collected. He was my partner when I eventually landed a paid job as an EMT/rescue technician.

Mike and I worked hand in hand, providing exceptional care to our patients without even having to say a word to each other. We just knew what the other needed before having to ask. Although we worked hard, we also had some of the best times and laughs together. These experiences helped me understand the importance of professionalism while not taking ourselves too seriously all the time, especially in moments of adversity.

Those days in the firehouse laid the foundation for the leader I'd become. Little did I know that these experiences would lead me down a path of service, medical training, and the power of teamwork—values that would shape my life.

At the time, these values didn't seem important; they were just part of my daily life. But looking back, they meant everything. They molded me into who I am today. This realization came to me over time; I just didn't see it then. But, as always, God had a plan.

Following my passion for firefighting, I decided to make it a career by becoming a certified EMT. I needed a job, and the financial realities of life pushed me to prioritize full-time work over a college degree. It was a tough decision, but it was necessary to pay the bills. I threw myself into my new role with enthusiasm. However, the financial rewards were minimal. In western Pennsylvania, a "paid" EMT made just ten dollars an hour.

Yeah, you read that right—ten bucks an hour. The sense of insignificance that had haunted me before started to creep back in. I worked tirelessly, often for twenty-four-hour shifts, only to leave one station and start another eight-hour job elsewhere. It felt like a never-ending cycle, an endless and futile effort with no real reward. The extensive training and huge responsibilities were all reduced to a meager hourly wage.

As I questioned the point of my relentless effort, my frustration grew. What was the purpose if I had nothing to show for it? Doubts about my path loomed large, and I felt completely lost. The obstacles and hardships seemed insurmountable, threatening to overwhelm my perseverance.

During this tough time, I found myself contemplating suicide. The darkness had crept in, and I felt engulfed by it. But with the grace of God and my unwavering faith, I managed to pull myself out of that dark place. That's when I realized I needed to change my life's direction. This phase of my journey was a stark reminder that there's always a glimmer of hope, a path to change, and a chance for redemption, even in the darkest times. It was a revelation that eventually led me to discover my true calling and the immense potential within me.

My Challenges and Setbacks

In my early twenties, life felt like I was wandering aimlessly, not sure where I was going or what I wanted to do. I worked hard, but it felt like I was stuck in a loop with no clear future. Then, out of nowhere, Julie came into my life and turned everything around.

Back then, I didn't have much faith in myself and wasn't sure where I was headed. I was skeptical about our relationship and hesitant to take it seriously, thinking I didn't have much to offer. Little did I know, our connection had so much more depth than I realized.

Julie and I talked a lot about education. We both had some college credits but never finished our degrees. Even though we had stable jobs, we knew there was more to strive for. So we decided to enroll in classes at our local community college, a decision that reignited a spark in me.

As I thought about going back to school, old worries and doubts resurfaced. Could I do it? My previous experiences with education hadn't been great, and uncertainty loomed large. But despite our reservations, Julie and I took the plunge and signed up for classes. Adult learning turned out to be eye-opening, and I quickly found a new passion for education. The challenges that had held me back for years became the fuel for a fire within me.

What started as a few community college classes led to a bachelor's degree from the University of California of Pennsylvania. My thirst for knowledge was back, and nothing could stop me. This journey didn't end there—I went on to earn a master's degree from the University of Ohio.

Let's be real, getting a college degree as an adult is tough. The nights are long, and the financial sacrifices are significant. I remember this humbling moment when my wife was in the hospital for the birth of our daughter. There I was, sitting with my laptop, finishing up an exam for one of my online classes. That's just how determined I was to make the most of every opportunity. My wife and I ended up having a beautiful baby girl, Hannah, and it was worth it all.

My family was my constant source of inspiration. I had an insatiable desire to achieve more, driven by the knowledge that my lack of formal education was holding me back. I refused to accept those limitations, and once I had those two degrees, the doors that opened were incredible.

Every sleepless night and every dollar spent was worth it. My message is simple: stop doubting yourself and leap. I know college isn't for everyone, but if something is holding you back, remove that obstacle and keep moving forward. For me, education was the barrier, and overcoming it made a huge difference in my life.

Remember, the pursuit of knowledge is a powerful force that can break down walls, shatter self-doubt, and open doors to an unimaginable future. It's never too late to chase your dreams, invest in yourself, and transform your life. Your journey starts with that first step, and it's one you'll never regret taking.

As I mentioned earlier, I spent a lot of time in public safety—a time in my life that still gets me excited. Those days taught me how to handle tough situations quickly and with determination.

Imagine a world where sirens are always blaring, fires are raging, and lives are on the line. As an EMS practitioner and firefighter, that was my reality early in my career. The first emergency call I responded to as a rookie EMS practitioner was a real test of my skills and nerves. I could hear my heartbeat pounding in my ears, but I knew I had to face the chaos head-on.

I felt a mix of unease and excitement as we rushed to the scene. It was like diving into the deep end, a trial by fire into the world of firefighting. I couldn't help but wonder—what was waiting for me? How would I handle whatever came next? This was the start of an experience that would seriously shape my career as a firefighter and leader.

The truck's engine roared to life as we sped to the call, adrenaline surging through my veins. It was a medical emergency, and when we got there, we found a patient in cardiac arrest. The air was thick with urgency and fear, demanding quick and precise action.

We jumped out of the truck, and the weight of responsibility hit me like a ton of bricks. My mind was racing, but I had to stay focused.

The team moved like a well-oiled machine, each person knowing exactly what to do. I watched in awe as they set up the equipment and started CPR.

Standing there with the other firefighters and medics, I felt like I was watching from the outside. These seasoned pros were working tirelessly to save the patient, their faces set with determination. They weren't just reacting; they were leading, taking charge of a chaotic situation and doing everything possible to save a life.

In that moment, I had a lightbulb moment about leadership. These guys weren't immune to fear—they were human. But they channeled that fear into a fierce drive to help. It hit me that real leadership is about embracing your vulnerabilities and using them to fuel your resolve.

Seeing the team's unwavering commitment in such a high-stress situation left a mark on me. Watching them handle the crisis with skill and empathy showed me that true leadership means being open to your vulnerabilities and letting them drive you forward. That moment became the cornerstone of my leadership philosophy, shaping my career as both a firefighter and a leader.

This encounter inspired me to lead by example. It wasn't about projecting invincibility; it was about acknowledging concerns and doubts and using them as catalysts for growth. As I advanced in my career, I realized that great leadership comes from a place of vulnerability. It involves admitting flaws, learning from mistakes, and showing that it's okay not to have all the answers.

This insight led to my commitment to vulnerable leadership—a style based on sincerity and empathy. It's about creating an environment where team members feel safe expressing their concerns and ideas, recognizing that their imperfections are vital contributions to success. I'll delve more into vulnerable leadership in a later chapter.

Life, like that pivotal moment during my first fire call, presents opportunities to turn obstacles into stepping-stones. By embracing vulnerability and using our anxieties as tools for progress, we become leaders who inspire, teammates who uplift, and individuals who endure the fiercest fires. It's a leadership journey ignited by the flames of vulnerability, driving us toward a more meaningful and effective life.

During moments of confusion and panic, I drew inspiration from an EMS colleague and the team. Their story of persisting against all odds became my guiding light as I cared for the injured and offered hope. My empathetic approach to people's needs, then and now, was born from these experiences.

Looking back, I see how each challenge and setback, each moment of doubt and perseverance, has shaped my path. The concept of vulnerable leadership was born from my experiences, teaching me that true strength lies in acknowledging our vulnerabilities and using them to connect, inspire, and lead others.

Life has a way of throwing curveballs, and it's through these trials that we discover our true potential. My journey through the fire department, the loss of dear friends, and the personal battles with self-doubt have all contributed to the leader I am today. Each obstacle became a stepping-stone, propelling me forward and teaching me invaluable lessons about resilience, empathy, and the power of vulnerability.

As we continue on this journey together, remember that adversity is not a roadblock but a teacher. It's in the darkest moments that we find our brightest strengths. Embrace your vulnerabilities, lean into your challenges, and let them guide you toward growth and transformation. The road ahead may be tough, but it's also full of opportunities to lead with purpose and heart. Together, we can navigate the storms, uplift each other, and create a legacy of compassion and strength.

CHAPTER 3

Resilience Unveiled: Shaping a Leader Through Trials

Excellence is not a singular act but a habit. You are what you repeatedly do. The trials and challenges you face are what shape you into a true leader. Embrace them, learn from them, and let them mold you into someone who can inspire others.
—Shaquille O'Neal

Life's got this intricate way of using tough times like a hammer and anvil, shaping us into resilient folks. As I wander back through the memories, it's crystal clear that these struggles have been the furnace where my leadership was forged. Every hurdle, setback, and win has molded me into the resilient leader I stand as today.

The Early Foundations of Resilience

My path to leadership wasn't a straight shot; it was more like a winding trail with plenty of bumps and unexpected turns. But each twist and challenge only made my resolve stronger and deepened my resilience.

From the get-go, life threw me curveballs. Battling chronic illness from a young age, I was often sidelined, feeling vulnerable and out of the loop. Hospital visits were the norm rather than the exception, but it was in these tough moments that the seeds of resilience started to sprout within me.

Those chaotic early years were tough, but they taught me valuable lessons in sticking it out and adapting on the fly. I learned to handle life's storms with a certain grace, to face the unknown with guts, and to see each challenge as a chance to grow. These experiences laid down the groundwork for the resilient leader I would become.

Navigating the Rapids: Challenges in Education and Career

Stepping into the world of education and later into my career, I faced new challenges that tested my resilience all over again. Learning disabilities and communication hurdles tried to knock me off my academic track, but I wasn't about to let my limitations define me.

Growing up with learning disabilities was no walk in the park. School was tough. I struggled with reading and writing, and it felt like my brain was always a step behind everyone else's. But honestly, the real test came when I decided to go back to school as an adult. I was a full-time EMT/firefighter, a newlywed, a new father, and a business owner. Juggling all that while battling a learning disability was like trying to climb a mountain with a backpack full of bricks.

Balancing work, family, and school was chaotic. I'd be up at night with the baby, head to work for a twenty-four-hour shift, and then try to squeeze in study time whenever I could. Reading through textbooks was a real grind. I'd have to go over the same paragraph multiple times just to make sense of it. Exams? Those felt like never-ending uphill battles.

Staying organized was a constant struggle. My notes were not structured at times, and I was always losing track of assignments. Time management was not easy. I had to learn how to juggle firefighting shifts, run my business, be there for my wife and kid, and somehow keep up with my studies. There were days when I felt completely overwhelmed, like I was drowning in responsibilities.

But I'm a stubborn guy, and I wasn't about to let my learning disabilities or any of these challenges define me. I sought out support, figured out new ways to learn, and adapted. I found strength in my ability to overcome these hurdles. Each setback became a chance to grow. Rejection and disappointment didn't knock me down for long; they fueled my determination to keep pushing forward.

The Forge of Adversity: Building Resilience in Leadership

Climbing the leadership ladder, I bumped into new and tougher challenges. Leading teams, dealing with complex office dynamics, and juggling multiple priorities—these tested my resilience in ways I hadn't faced before.

It was in these leadership trials that I truly grasped the power of resilience. I learned to lead not just with boldness but also with heart, to tackle adversity gracefully, and to inspire others to do the same. By being open about my vulnerabilities, I built real connections with my team, empowering us to tackle challenges together.

When uncertainty and tough times hit, I leaned on my past battles, drawing on those resilience lessons that had shaped me. I saw failures as learning moments, not roadblocks, viewing them as steps toward greater success.

Through it all, I stayed true to leading with integrity and empathy, understanding that real resilience means not just bouncing back but also growing stronger through the trials.

The Legacy of Resilience: Inspiring Others to Lead

Reflecting on my path, I'm really struck by how my ability to keep bouncing back has not only carried me through but also touched those around me. As a leader, I've tried to foster a resilient spirit within my team, encouraging them to meet challenges with bravery and resolve. I always tell my employees, mentees, and audiences at my speaking events, "The best of you comes out through your failures. Do not run from your failures, but learn from them." I've shared my own rough patches, using them to teach and inspire, and I've seen the ripple effect of resilience. It's amazing to watch people overcome tough odds and achieve things they thought were out of reach, and to know that resilience isn't just a personal trait but a catalyst for positive change.

For instance, I've seen nurses working double shifts during a pandemic, still managing to provide top-notch care with a smile. They push through their own fatigue and stress because they know their patients rely on them.

Another example is witnessing a patient who was given a slim chance of recovery after a severe accident, defy the odds. With the unwavering support of the medical team and their own determination, they not only recovered but went on to lead a full, active life. Seeing doctors, nurses, and therapists rally around that patient, providing medical care and emotional support, showcased the true power of resilience and teamwork.

These experiences highlight that resilience isn't just about bouncing back; it's about pushing forward, inspiring others, and making a real difference even in the toughest situations.

Looking to the Future: Embracing Resilience in a Changing World

Looking ahead, I'm aware of the challenges that come with a constantly shifting world. But I'm confident in my resilience and ability to handle whatever comes my way. My past has equipped me well to thrive in an ever-changing landscape. I'm ready to face the unknown, to tackle adversity head-on, and to lead with courage and conviction.

Continuing on this leadership journey, I'm committed to inspiring others to tap into their own resilience and unlock their potential. After all, it's our resilience that will see us through tough times and lead us to brighter days. As we move forward together, I can't wait to see the amazing things we'll achieve, powered by resilience and the firm belief that anything is possible.

The future might be unpredictable, but that's what makes it exciting. I know there will be bumps in the road and unexpected twists, but I'm not worried. I've faced enough challenges to know that I can handle whatever life throws at me. My past has taught me how to adapt and keep pushing forward, no matter what.

I'm not just focused on my own resilience, though. I want to help others find their inner strength too. Whether it's my team at work, my mentees, or people at my speaking events, I'm dedicated to showing others that they can overcome their obstacles and achieve great things. It's all about believing in yourself and not being afraid to fail. Remember, the best of you comes out through your failures. Do not run from your failures, but learn from them.

As we move forward together, I'm excited to see what we can accomplish. With resilience as our foundation, I believe we can tackle any challenge and come out stronger on the other side. The world is full of opportunities waiting to be seized, and I'm ready to lead the charge.

So here's to the future, with all its uncertainties and possibilities. Let's embrace it with open arms, face our challenges head-on, and keep pushing the boundaries of what we can achieve. Together, there's nothing we can't handle.

CHAPTER 4

Turning Scars into Leadership Gold

God never wastes a hurt! In fact, your greatest ministry will most likely come out of your greatest hurt.
—Rick Warren

Let's talk about the darker parts of my life's soundtrack—the tough times with mental health that have been like a recurring somber tune echoing in my mind. This chapter is all about stepping into those shadows and showing the raw, real side of struggling with depression, anxiety, and even thoughts of ending it all. But it's also about how I found a way out—a melody of faith that pulled me from the depths and into the light.

It all started back in my teens, with a constant background music of self-doubt and feeling worthless. Depression was like this heavy blanket thrown over everything, darkening my thoughts and actions. Anxiety chimed in too, creating a constant buzz that drowned out any happiness.

At my lowest, thoughts of suicide crept in, playing a dark tune that suggested an escape from the battles raging inside. I felt like a tiny whisper lost in the chaos of life, completely overwhelmed by what seemed like a never-ending series of personal failures.

In those darkest times, the pain seemed never-ending, and it felt like the world was totally oblivious to the silent, painful tune playing inside me. I desperately wanted to be seen, to have someone recognize the struggle, but feeling so alone only made the despair louder. Fighting this battle against the darkness within felt like facing an unbeatable enemy, with every visible and invisible scar telling a story of brokenness.

Faith as My Firm Foundation

Just when the shadows felt like they might swallow me whole, a new sound softly joined the tune—faith. At first, it was just a faint whisper, almost drowned out by the despair, but slowly it started to get louder and resonate within me.

Faith began to shine like a guiding star through my darkest nights. It wasn't a quick fix, but slowly, it brought the realization that there was more than just the darkness. In quiet moments of prayer and reflection, I started to find peace. The songs of faith gently healed the wounds that once felt way too deep.

Faith shifted the way I saw my struggles. It turned my story around, letting me view my past hurts not as marks of defeat, but as badges of resilience. The endless loop of self-doubt in my head began to quiet down as faith whispered affirmations of my worth and purpose.

As this redemption song grew stronger, faith overpowered the jarring chords of anxiety and depression. I found my strength, not because the struggles disappeared, but because I believed I could rise above them. Faith directed this turnaround, guiding me from deep despair to discovering who I really am.

Faith turned into more than just a background note—it became the driving beat pushing me forward. It laid down a solid base for rebuilding the shattered parts of myself. As the darkness lifted, I started to accept my scars and vulnerabilities with a new grace.

In this faith-filled journey, I found a support system that wasn't just about the people I could see but also included a higher presence that watched over my journey, witnessing every fall and celebrating every rise.

What used to be a haunting soundtrack of despair in my struggle with mental health transformed into a powerful anthem of resilience and renewal. The scars that once played painful notes now harmonized a melody of strength. Faith rewrote my dark, chaotic tunes into a calm, soothing melody.

Looking back, I see that faith wasn't a magic eraser for all the tough stuff but a guiding tune that helped me navigate through the mess in my head. Through faith, I found the courage to face the darkest times, the strength to deal with my vulnerabilities, and the toughness to come out a survivor.

As the music of my life plays on, faith keeps on being the anthem through every high and low. It's the unwritten melody woven through my existence, reminding me that even in the darkest moments, there's always a tune of hope ready to play.

Embracing Vulnerability as a Source of Strength

Vulnerability gets a bad rap. It's often seen as a crack in the armor, something leaders should avoid. But here's the thing—I've learned that it's actually a superpower. Opening up, showing the real you, is what builds real connections and trust in a team.

Take my battle with mental health, for example. Those dark days filled with anxiety and depression made me feel totally alone, swallowed up by a sea of self-doubt and despair. But the game changed when I started to open up about what I was going through.

Picture this: It's one of those gloomy evenings, rain tapping against the window like it's trying to drum in the chaos inside my head. There I was, sitting alone, feeling like the weight of the world was on my shoulders. My mind was a whirlwind of negative thoughts, each one a punch to my self-esteem.

In that raw moment, I made a choice that turned things around. I picked up the phone, hands shaking, and spilled everything to a friend I trusted deeply. I didn't hold back my tears or my words. I let it all out. "I feel like I'm drowning," I admitted, my voice breaking. "Every day is a struggle, and I don't know how to keep going. I'm terrified that I'm not enough, that I'm failing at everything."

The response? It was nothing short of a lifeline. Instead of judgment, I got a whole lot of empathy and understanding. My friend listened, really listened, providing a safe space for me to let go of the mess tangled up inside. "Josh, I'm so sorry you're going through this," he said, their voice filled with concern. "But you need to know that you're not alone. We all have our battles, and it's okay to feel this way. You don't have to be perfect."

That conversation was a turning point. It taught me that I wasn't alone, that others cared, and that sharing my struggle could actually lift some of the burden off my shoulders. That night, vulnerability showed me its strength, and it's a lesson I've carried with me ever since.

So here's a shout-out to anyone feeling bottled up—let it out. Be real and share the tough stuff. You're not alone, and you might just find that others are ready to stand with you in your darkest times.

Turning Pain into Purpose

Our past hurts can shape our future in big ways. My own struggles with mental health have turned me into a champion for servant leadership, constantly pushing me to use what I've learned to help others.

In those really tough times, it might be hard to see any light ahead. But it's often in these low points that we find our true calling. For me, it was realizing that my battles could help me understand and support others in similar fights.

As a leader, I'm all about creating a workplace that really cares about mental and emotional well-being. I'm here to support and provide resources for those who are struggling, and I'm committed to building a space where everyone feels respected and valued.

Mental health is crucial to me as a leader because it profoundly impacts every aspect of our lives. When mental health is prioritized, it leads to improved employee engagement, higher productivity, and a more positive workplace culture. By acknowledging and addressing mental health, we can break the stigma and create an environment where people feel safe to express their needs and seek help.

In my leadership journey, I've learned that vulnerability is not a weakness but a powerful tool to connect with others. Sharing my own experiences with mental health has allowed me to build deeper relationships and foster trust within my team. It shows that it's okay to struggle and that seeking help is a sign of strength, not weakness.

By prioritizing mental health, we can create a culture of empathy and support that not only benefits individuals but also strengthens the entire organization. When people feel seen, heard, and valued, they are more likely to thrive both personally and professionally. As a leader, my goal is to ensure that mental health remains a top priority, fostering a work environment where everyone can reach their full potential.

Transforming Scars into Strengths

Every scar from our past helps shape us as leaders. My own journey through mental health challenges has taught me resilience, taught me empathy, and showed me the importance of keeping it real—qualities I bring into my leadership every day.

Faith has been my guide through it all, helping me face my past, embrace my vulnerabilities, and find purpose in my pain.

As I keep going on this leadership path, I'm reminded that our scars aren't just reminders of our battles; they're proof of our victories. By owning our stories and using them to grow, we unlock our true potential as leaders, ready to make a real difference. With faith, openness, and a dedication to serving others, we can turn our toughest trials into our greatest strengths.

In sharing the darker parts of my personal journey, I hope to shine a light on the power of vulnerability and faith in overcoming life's most challenging moments. My struggles with mental health—those haunting tunes of depression, anxiety, and thoughts of giving up—were not the end of my story but the beginning of a profound transformation. Faith became my guiding melody, leading me out of the shadows and helping me to see my scars as badges of resilience rather than marks of defeat. Through opening up and embracing vulnerability, I found strength and a support system that made all the difference. These experiences have shaped me into a leader committed to prioritizing mental health and fostering a culture of empathy and support. As I continue my journey, I carry with me the knowledge that our toughest trials can become our greatest strengths, guiding us toward a future filled with hope, purpose, and unwavering resilience.

CHAPTER 5

Nurturing Growth and Empowering Others

Happiness doesn't result from what we get, but from what we give. True empowerment comes from lifting others up and helping them realize their potential.
—Ben Carson

Leadership is a lot like conducting a symphony—it's all about getting those different notes to work together to make something amazing. In this chapter, we'll dive into how our thoughts and beliefs can shape our own paths and lift others to awesome heights. Plus, we'll talk about why finding a mentor is super important for your growth.

Think of our mindset like a blank canvas. It's ready and waiting for us to throw on some vibrant colors and bold strokes. As we peel back layer by layer, we see how our thoughts can be shaped, shifted, and steered to unlock our full potential as leaders. And this isn't just about being a big shot in the boardroom; it's about tackling challenges, bouncing back from letdowns, and crafting our own success stories.

Unlocking the Power of Mentorship: Essential for Personal Growth

Alright, let's dive into the whole mentor thing. Seriously, having a mentor can be a total game-changer for your life and career. But I get it—figuring out how to find one and understanding what they should do can be confusing. So, let's break it down in a straightforward, no-nonsense way.

How to Find a Mentor
Look Around You:
Start with your immediate circles—your workplace, industry events, LinkedIn, or even your community. Sometimes, the best mentors are people you already know but haven't thought of asking.

Network, Network, Network:
Attend events, join professional groups, and be active on platforms like LinkedIn. Don't just show up; engage with people. Ask questions, share your experiences, and see who resonates with your goals and values.

Ask Directly:
Once you've identified someone who could be a great mentor, don't be shy. Reach out with a clear message. Something like, "Hey, I admire your work and would love to learn from you. Would you be open to mentoring me?"

Be Specific:
When asking, be specific about what you're looking for. Do you need career advice, help with a particular skill, or just someone to bounce ideas off of? Clear expectations help both of you understand the commitment.

What a Mentor Should Do
Share Wisdom:
A mentor's job is to share their experiences, both the successes and the mistakes. You get to learn from their journey and avoid some of the pitfalls they faced.

Offer Guidance:
They help you navigate your career path, offering advice on tough decisions and helping you set realistic and ambitious goals.

Be a Sounding Board:
Sometimes, you just need someone to listen and provide feedback. A good mentor will listen without judgment and offer constructive criticism.

Challenge You:
A mentor isn't just there to pat you on the back. They should push you out of your comfort zone, challenge your thinking, and encourage you to grow.

Provide Accountability:
They help you stay on track with your goals. Knowing you have someone to report your progress to can be a strong motivator.

Making the Most of Your Mentorship
Be Proactive:
Don't wait for your mentor to reach out. Take the initiative to schedule meetings, ask questions, and seek feedback.

Be Respectful:
Value their time and insights. Show up prepared for your meetings and be respectful of their advice, even if you don't always agree.

Be Open:
Be open to feedback, even if it's tough to hear. Growth happens outside your comfort zone.

Finding and working with a mentor can truly accelerate your personal and professional growth. So, get out there, connect with people, and find that mentor who can help you reach new heights!

Pushing Forward: Embracing Change and Seizing Opportunities

"Pushing forward" became my motto, guiding me through the twists and turns of life. I had a fulfilling career in business development, a wonderful family, and a good life. Yet the relentless question of "What's next?" kept nagging at me. As I set my sights on becoming a regional business development director, the possibility of relocation became a potential game changer.

Navigating the delicate conversation about uprooting our settled lives was tricky. But I discovered the transformative effect of being open to possibilities. My business mentor, Patrick, threw a curveball at me one day. He presented the prospect of becoming a CEO—a role that seemed like a distant dream. The catch? It required relocation.

At first, the idea of becoming a CEO felt out of reach. But the more I thought about it, the more the potential excited me. With Patrick's encouragement, I started to see the opportunity in a new light. I realized that sometimes, the biggest leaps forward require a willingness to embrace change and step into the unknown.

Faith, resilience, and an openness to change became my guiding lights. I leaned on my faith to give me the courage to take the leap. Resilience helped me navigate the challenges and uncertainties that came with such a big decision. And staying open to change allowed me to see the possibilities instead of just the risks.

So, before I even hit forty, I found myself embracing the CEO position. Can you believe it? It was a pivotal chapter in my life, one that was shaped by adaptability and the willingness to take a chance on something new. Moving my family and starting this new adventure was no small feat, but it taught me that pushing forward often means stepping out of your comfort zone and believing in the potential of what lies ahead.

This journey wasn't just about a career move; it was about personal growth and discovering what I was truly capable of. It reaffirmed my belief that we all have the power to shape our own paths if we're willing to push forward, embrace change, and seize the opportunities that come our way.

Practical Strategies for Shifting Your Mindset

Moving from a mindset of self-doubt and scarcity to one of empowerment and abundance has been a game changer, and here are some real-deal strategies that might help you too.

Cultivate Self-Awareness: Start by really paying attention to your thoughts, your feelings, and how you react to things. Get to know the patterns that might be holding you back.

Challenge Your Inner Critic: Got negative thoughts? Challenge them with some positive truths about yourself. It's about changing the tapes that play in your head.

Celebrate Your Wins: Big or small, make a big deal out of your victories. It builds confidence and keeps you motivated.

Practice Gratitude Daily: Every day, make a note of things you're thankful for. It shifts your focus from what you lack to what you have.

Surround Yourself with Positivity: Hang out with people who lift you up, and soak up content that inspires you.

Set Realistic Goals: Break those big dreams down into steps you can actually tackle. It keeps you going and makes the big things seem less daunting.

Lean into Vulnerability: Don't be afraid to share your struggles. It builds connections, and you'd be surprised how much support you might find.

Learn from Setbacks: Instead of beating yourself up over a failure, look at what it can teach you.

Visualize Success: Spend some time picturing yourself smashing your goals. It can boost your belief in what's possible.

Practice Self-Compassion: Be as kind to yourself as you would be to a friend in the same boat.

Focus on Abundance: Keep your eyes on your own path and what you've achieved instead of getting stuck on what others are doing.

Practice Mindful Self-Talk: Keep the way you talk to yourself positive. It can change the way you feel and act.

Challenge Comfort Zones: Push yourself to try new things. It's how you grow.

Learn and Adapt: Stay curious and open to new experiences. It's all about being flexible and ready for whatever comes your way.

Set Healthy Boundaries: It's okay to say no sometimes, to choose what really matters to you.

Switching from a mindset of scarcity to one of abundance isn't overnight magic—it's a journey. Take it one step at a time, be easy on yourself, and grab hold of every chance to lead with authenticity and an open heart.

As we look to the future, remember that our mindset shapes our reality. By nurturing growth and empowering others, we create a ripple effect of positivity and strength. Here's to embracing change, pushing forward, and seizing every opportunity with resilience and courage. Together, there's nothing we can't achieve. Let's go out there and make it happen.

CHAPTER 6

Riding the Rollercoaster of Success and Setbacks

Life is full of setbacks. Success is determined by how you handle them. With faith, perseverance, and the right attitude, every setback c an become a stepping-stone to greater things.
—Franklin Graham

Life's journey is anything but straight. It's full of twists, turns, and the occasional loop-de-loop. I've navigated my own winding path through leadership and self-discovery, with a mix of high wins and some pretty humbling lows. Let's dive into what it means to make real progress, how resilience truly shapes us, and why perseverance is a game changer.

A New Leadership Journey: Lessons and Challenges

From being the odd one out in elementary school to finding my feet in high school, my early years were tough but formative. I dealt with plenty of teasing and moments of self-doubt, but a few key people believed in me and gave me the push I needed to see that I could be more. These experiences taught me that true leadership is built on empathy, understanding, and the guts to face up against the tough stuff.

Resilience Forged in Adversity

By the time I hit fourth grade, I was really testing my academic and personal mettle. The challenges I faced—whether from classmates or unsupportive teachers—taught me to stand firm and not let adversity silence me. I turned these trials into opportunities to grow tougher and more resilient. It became clear that leadership isn't just about winning; it's about learning how to turn obstacles into stepping-stones.

Fresh Insights and Challenges

Looking back, a few lessons stand out:

Empathy as a Leadership Tool: Having been on the receiving end of ridicule, I learned to recognize and uplift others who are struggling.

Adversity as a Teacher: Tough times taught me that challenges are powerful teachers. Embracing them as opportunities to learn makes you stronger.

Inclusive Leadership: Being part of a special-needs program showed me the importance of not leaving anyone behind. True leadership means ensuring everyone is supported and included.

Self-Doubt as a Catalyst: I experienced ongoing self-doubt through high school, but I used it as motivation to prove my worth and help others do the same.

New Challenges for Aspiring Leaders

For those stepping up to lead, consider these pointers:

Cultivate Resilience: See setbacks as temporary and build toughness by viewing them as challenges to conquer, not roadblocks.

Embrace Diversity: Value diverse perspectives and make sure everyone on your team feels seen, heard, and respected.

Support the Vulnerable: Reach out to those who feel isolated or misunderstood, offering mentorship and support.

Reframe Self-Doubt: Use self-doubt as fuel to drive improvement and personal growth.

Leadership Journey: Success and Pressure Intertwined
Stepping into my hospital CEO shoes, I quickly learned that success comes bundled with pressure. Balancing the needs and visions of different people in the organization, managing expectations, and honoring the hospital's legacy required a delicate touch. Success wasn't just about hitting targets; it was about mastering personal challenges under pressure.

Lessons in Resilience and Overcoming Setbacks

Life has schooled me well in turning vulnerabilities into strengths, transforming setbacks into motivation, and celebrating the small wins along with the big ones. These lessons have taught me that setbacks don't define us; they propel us forward, offering golden opportunities for growth.

Skepticism, like that pesky guest who crashes your party and questions everything you do, often pops up in leadership. It's that nagging voice questioning your skills, doubting your goals, and planting seeds of uncertainty. But just like every challenge I've faced on this wild ride, skepticism has been a stepping-stone, sparking growth and showcasing the might of grit.

Whenever a new opportunity, an ambitious goal, or a bold vision comes up, the doubters aren't far behind. They'll furrow their brows, raise their eyebrows, and mutter, "Really? Can you do this?" They'll say, "Hold up, that's not how things are done." But here's the scoop: skepticism, whether it's from others or within yourself, is a bridge, not a barrier. It's what links the land of doubts to the realm of possibilities.

Life often teaches us about ourselves at the most unexpected moments, lighting up our paths during deep self-discovery. My journey to leadership was no different, shaped by transformative experiences that forged my drive and passion in the face of adversity.

Entrepreneurial Ventures

Ever walked into a coffee shop, breathed in the aroma of fresh coffee, and thought about owning one? Or have you ever juggled a day job with a side hustle and then thought of starting another business? If so, you're not alone, and it's clear you've got that entrepreneurial spirit. I've always had a knack for diving into new ventures, turning passions into projects, and embracing life's complexities.

Early on, I got hooked on medical sales, which led me to start Saving Grace Medical. This venture focused on selling automated external defibrillators and providing crucial CPR and first aid training. For about thirteen years, I balanced this side gig with my main job, soaking up entrepreneurship and the art of multitasking.

But the entrepreneurial bug is relentless. When I spotted a gap in the market for a staffing agency, I jumped on it. I co-founded Mountainview Staffing with a buddy, aiming to match job seekers with meaningful work. Although our time with Mountainview Staffing was short-lived, it taught me a ton about resilience and adapting in the business world.

Then there's my latest gig, Viewpoint Leadership and Development Company. This venture became the perfect outlet for my passion for leadership. I envisioned a place where I could share my professional and personal journey, inspire others with my experiences, and foster growth in individuals and organizations.

I love having options, pursuing various interests, and accepting life's challenges. Although running my hospital is my primary focus, these diverse roles and businesses feed my passions and provide continuous opportunities for growth and joy. Entrepreneurship lets us chase our dreams in so many ways—it's not always smooth sailing, but it's the journey that counts.

Reflecting on this chapter, I see that true leadership isn't about sailing smoothly; it's about steering the ship through storms and coming out stronger. The ups and downs have shaped me not only into a CEO but also into a leader who's been forged in the crucible of both success and pressure. As this journey continues, I'm thankful for every lesson, every bit of resilience I've built, and the unwavering belief in the power of bouncing back.

CHAPTER 7

The Compass of Transformative Leadership and Cultivating Your Core Values

*Leadership is not about titles, positions, or flowcharts.
It is about one life influencing another.*
—John C. Maxwell

Picture this: you're the captain of a ship, sailing through unknown waters. The stars are hidden behind clouds, and the sea is rough. Without a compass, you're just guessing which way to go. Leading without knowing your personal core values feels a lot like this. Your values are the compass guiding you through the turbulent seas of decision-making, challenges, and triumphs. Let's dive into how identifying and cultivating your core values can transform your leadership journey.

The Compass Found

Envision yourself as the newly appointed CEO of a hospital. You're smart, driven, and full of ideas, but you're also overwhelmed. Your calendar is packed with meetings, and your team looks to you for guidance on every decision. You're constantly putting out fires, feeling like you're steering a ship without a map.

One evening, after another long day, you sit in your office, staring at the city lights. You realize you need a clearer sense of direction. Your mentor once told you, "You need to find your compass. Your core values will guide you through anything." It's time to figure out what that means.

You decide to take your mentor's advice to heart. You begin by reflecting on your past. You think about the times you felt most proud and the moments when you felt out of sync with yourself. One memory stands out: a few years ago, you stood up to a senior executive who wanted to cut corners on a patient care initiative. Despite the pressure, you refused to compromise on quality. This memory reminds you of how much you value integrity.

Next, you consider the people you admire. Your former boss, who always led with transparency, and your grandmother, who taught you the importance of compassion, are at the top of your list. These reflections point you toward honesty and compassion as core values.

You then tune into your gut feelings. You feel most alive when you're innovating, pushing boundaries, and encouraging your team to think creatively. Conversely, you feel drained when stuck in bureaucratic red tape. Innovation is clearly a core value for you.

But there's more to your values than just the high points and inspirations. You realize your values are also shaped by some painful experiences and old wounds. You remember your first job, where you were frequently undermined and dismissed by a toxic manager. The frustration and hurt you felt during that time crystallized your belief in the importance of respect and empowerment.

Another pivotal moment was when you lost a close friend because of a misunderstanding and lack of communication. The pain of that loss made you value transparency and open communication even more. You don't want anyone else to experience the kind of hurt you had.

These wounds, while painful, had carved deep values into your psyche. They weren't just scars; they were reminders of what you wanted to stand for as a leader.

Living the Values

With your core values identified—integrity, honesty, compassion, innovation, respect, and transparency—you feel a renewed sense of purpose. But identifying them is just the first step. Living them is where the real transformation happens.

One day, a major mistake in a project surfaces, threatening a critical patient relationship. You have two choices: cover it up and hope it doesn't come to light or own up to it immediately. Guided by your value of honesty, you call a meeting, explain the situation, and work with your team to find a solution. Your transparency not only preserves the patient's trust but also strengthens your team's respect for you.

In another instance, you notice one of your top nurses, Emma, is unusually quiet and distracted. Instead of reprimanding her for missed deadlines, you take Emma aside and ask if everything is all right. Emma confides that she's going through a tough time at home. Drawing on your value of compassion, you offer support, adjust Emma's workload, and connect her with hospital resources. This act of kindness not only helps Emma but also shows the entire team that you value them as individuals.

Your commitment to innovation is evident in how you manage brainstorming sessions. You encourage your team to share wild ideas without fear of judgment. When one of their experimental projects fails, instead of reprimanding the team, you celebrate their efforts and the lessons learned. This approach fosters a culture of creativity and resilience.

Staying true to your values isn't always easy. There are moments of intense pressure and temptation to take the easy way out. But you know that compromising your values, even once, could undermine everything you're trying to build.

To keep yourself aligned, you make time for regular reflection. Every Friday, you spend an hour reviewing your week, considering whether your actions aligned with your core values. You also seek feedback from your team, encouraging them to hold you accountable. This practice not only reinforces your commitment but also demonstrates that you value their perspectives.

Think of your core values like muscles. The more you exercise them, the stronger they get. As the CEO of your hospital, you start small, embedding your values into your daily routine.

Every morning, you begin with a simple ritual: making rounds in the hospital, greeting every staff member and asking how they're doing. This isn't just small talk; it's your way of living your value of compassion. You know that by showing genuine interest in your team's well-being, you're building a supportive and trusting environment.

Your team is always watching you. How you act in tough situations speaks volumes about your true values. When a major issue with patient care arises, you have a choice: sweep it under the rug or be transparent about the challenges.

You choose transparency. You call a meeting with your staff and lay everything out. You admit the mistakes and share the reasons behind them, then you open the floor for solutions. This isn't just about fixing the problem; it's about showing your team that honesty and collaboration are non-negotiables.

It's not enough for you to live by your values; you need to instill them in your team. Start sharing your personal story more often—

how past experiences shaped your values of integrity, honesty, compassion, and innovation.

During an all-hands meeting, talk about your early career and the toxic work environment you once faced, which taught you the importance of respect. Share how losing a close friend to a misunderstanding underscored the need for transparency. These aren't just anecdotes; they're the foundation of the culture you want to build.

Hiring becomes a crucial part of your strategy. You're not just looking for skills; you're looking for values alignment. During interviews, ask candidates about their biggest challenges and how they handled them, trying to get a sense of their personal values.

One time, you hire a nurse named Alex. Alex isn't just talented; he has a passion for patient care and a deep respect for honest communication. He fits right in with the team and quickly becomes a driving force for new patient care initiatives, reinforcing the culture you're cultivating.

Cultivating values isn't a solo act. Encourage your team to recognize and reward each other when they see values in action. One day, Emma, who had once been quiet and distracted, steps up to lead a patient care project with incredible compassion and effectiveness. Make sure to highlight Emma's efforts in the next team meeting, reinforcing the importance of compassion and leadership.

Living your values isn't a one-and-done deal. It's an ongoing journey that requires regular reflection and adjustment. Every month, set aside time for a personal check-in. Think about your actions and decisions, considering whether they align with your core values.

Sometimes, you find areas where you've fallen short. Instead of beating yourself up, use these moments as learning opportunities. Encourage your team to give you feedback, creating an open dialogue about your collective commitment to the hospital's core values.

The Ripple Effect

Over time, you notice a change. Your team is more cohesive, motivated, and loyal. They trust your decisions and are inspired by your authenticity. The hospital's culture transforms, becoming more innovative and compassionate. Patients notice the difference too, praising the hospital for its integrity and transparency.

Your journey isn't without its challenges, but by identifying and living by your core values, you become a more effective, respected, and successful leader. Your values are your compass, guiding you through the stormy seas and helping you navigate toward a brighter future.

Cultivating your core values is a journey, not a destination. It takes time, effort, and commitment. But the payoff? It's huge. You'll become a leader who inspires, motivates, and transforms not just your team, but your entire organization. So keep those values front and center. Live them, share them, and nurture them every day. Remember, you're not just leading a team; you're shaping a culture and creating a legacy. And that's pretty awesome.

To help you on this journey, there's a workbook included at the back of the book specifically designed to assist you with this chapter. This workbook offers practical exercises, reflective prompts, and actionable steps to reinforce your understanding and application of core values in your leadership role.

CHAPTER 8

My Personal Core Values: Embracing Vulnerability, Empathy, Grace, Authenticity, and Humility

True leadership is about vulnerability and authenticity. It's about showing your true self and inspiring others to do the same.
—Tony Robbins

Leadership isn't about putting on a perfect facade. It's about showing up as your real self, flaws and all, and creating an environment where everyone feels safe to do the same. In this chapter, I'll share my personal core values, recount stories of how these values have shaped my leadership, and provide a guide on how to be a vulnerable leader. For me, that means leading with vulnerability, empathy, grace, authenticity, and humility—values that define how I live and lead my teams. When it comes to leadership, I believe in keeping it real and being human. These core values are the backbone of how I live my life and lead my teams. Let me break it down for you.

Leading with Vulnerability

First up, vulnerability. Yeah, it can be scary to let your guard down and be open with others, especially as a leader. But trust me, it's worth it.

Showing vulnerability isn't a sign of weakness; it's actually a strength. It builds trust and creates deeper connections with your team. When they see you're human and not some unapproachable boss, they'll be more likely to open up and bring their best selves to work.

Embracing Empathy

Next is empathy. This one's all about understanding and sharing the feelings of others. It's about really listening and trying to see things from someone else's perspective. When you lead with empathy, you create a supportive environment where people feel valued and understood. It's a game changer for building strong, cohesive teams.

Grace Under Pressure

Grace might seem like an old-fashioned word, but it's crucial in leadership. It's about staying calm, composed, and kind, even when the going gets tough. Leading with grace means handling conflicts and challenges with a level head and treating everyone with respect, no matter the situation. It's not always easy, but it's always worth it.

Authenticity Matters

Authenticity is all about being true to yourself. No one likes a phony, and your team can spot insincerity a mile away. Be yourself—scars and all. When you're authentic, you create a culture of honesty and transparency. Your team will appreciate your realness and feel more comfortable being themselves too.

Staying Humble

Last but definitely not least, humility. No matter how high you climb, it's essential to stay grounded and remember where you came from. Humility is about recognizing that you don't have all the answers and that you can always learn from others. It's about giving credit where it's due and lifting others up.

Personal Experiences
Navigating Changing Times
As a young CEO, I found myself at a crossroads. The world was changing, and so were the generations within our workforce. Traditional leadership just wasn't cutting it anymore. At a leadership seminar, a guest speaker talked about the evolving dynamics of the modern workplace, emphasizing the need to adapt to a multigenerational workforce. This hit home for me. I realized my leadership style had to evolve to meet these changing needs.

Understanding a Diverse Workforce
As a forward-thinking CEO, I dove into understanding our diverse workforce—from Gen X and millennials to emerging Gen Z employees. It became clear that vulnerability was key, especially for the younger generations who valued openness, authenticity, and emotional intelligence.

To lead effectively, I had to connect on a deeper level. I started sharing my own stories of successes and failures, showing my team that I was just as human as they were. For instance, I once shared about a time when I made a costly mistake early in my career. I talked about the lessons I learned and how it helped me grow. This kind of openness showed my team that it's okay to make mistakes as long as we learn from them.

Creating a Culture of Trust
I encouraged open dialogue, inviting everyone to share their ideas and concerns freely. One of the best decisions I made was to implement regular team meetings where everyone could voice their thoughts.

During these meetings, I made sure to listen more than I spoke. This created a culture of trust and collaboration, where everyone felt valued.

Empathy in Action

Empathy became a cornerstone of my leadership approach. I made it a point to really listen to my team's concerns. For example, during a particularly stressful project, I noticed a team member was struggling. Instead of pushing her harder, I took her aside for a one-on-one chat. I listened to her concerns and offered support. We rearranged her workload to better fit her strengths and needs. This not only helped the individual but also boosted overall team morale.

Embracing Grace in Leadership

Leading with grace means keeping your cool even when things get tough. During a rough financial quarter, instead of freaking out, I got the team together and laid out the situation honestly. We brainstormed solutions together, and I made sure to acknowledge everyone's contributions. This collective effort not only helped us get through the rough patch but also brought us closer as a team.

Grace is like that subtle but powerful thread that ties everything together. It's not just about being nice; it's about showing compassion, even when it's hard. It's about creating an atmosphere where people feel genuinely supported and valued, no matter what.

Living out grace as a leader means showing real compassion in everyday interactions. It's about understanding that everyone is fighting their own battles and recognizing their humanity. It's about seeing each team member as a person first, which can deeply influence how they perform and engage at work.

A big part of grace is forgiveness. It means seeing mistakes as chances for growth rather than just failures. Leaders who practice grace create a culture where people aren't afraid to try new things, mess up, and learn. This kind of environment not only frees people from the fear of failure but also encourages a more dynamic, innovative team spirit.

Grace doesn't just affect individuals—it shapes the whole team culture. A leader who leads with grace strives to make his or her team a safe space for everyone to express themselves and share their challenges openly. This kind of openness is crucial for building real trust and collaboration.

Empathy is at the heart of grace. It's about feeling what your team feels and experiencing things from their perspective. This deeper understanding can help leaders make more informed, considerate decisions that really support their team's well-being and productivity.

Graceful leadership means viewing challenges as opportunities to grow, not just obstacles. Leaders who embrace this perspective help their teams face difficulties with optimism and resilience, transforming potential setbacks into valuable learning moments.

True grace in leadership comes with a big dose of humility. Humble leaders are open about their flaws, seek out others' opinions, and genuinely appreciate everyone's contributions. This humility fosters a collaborative, inclusive work environment where everyone feels valued.

How leaders communicate can deeply affect their team. Graceful communication involves choosing words thoughtfully and providing feedback kindly, which can significantly boost team morale and motivation.

Graceful leaders take the time to build and nurture positive, supportive relationships within their team. They recognize and play to people's strengths and are there to support them when needed, which helps build a loyal, motivated team.

Another key aspect of grace in leadership is empowerment. Graceful leaders don't just support their team; they actively look for ways to help them grow, shine, and reach their full potential. This not only helps individuals advance but also drives the whole team forward. Appreciating and celebrating each team member's contributions is a fundamental part of leading with grace. Leaders who foster a culture of appreciation make everyone feel like a vital part of the team, which can greatly enhance overall team spirit and engagement.

Authenticity in Leadership
Being authentic is about being true to yourself and your values. I made a conscious effort to be transparent and genuine in all my interactions. During hospital-wide meetings, I shared not just our successes but also our struggles. I talked about the tough decisions we had to make and the rationale behind them. This transparency helped build trust and made my leadership more relatable.

Humility in Practice
Humility involves recognizing that you don't have all the answers and being open to learning from others. I actively sought feedback from my team, peers, and mentors, and used it to improve my leadership style. For example, after receiving feedback about my communication style being too directive, I worked on being more collaborative and inclusive in decision-making processes. This shift not only improved team dynamics but also led to better decision-making as diverse perspectives were considered.

Empowering the Team
I also focused on empowering my team. I started delegating more responsibilities and trusted them to take ownership of their projects. I provided the support they needed but didn't micromanage. This not only boosted their confidence but also allowed me to focus on strategic

initiatives. One of the best outcomes was seeing team members step up and take on leadership roles within their projects.

The Benefits
The benefit was incredible. Team morale improved, and we became more adaptable and responsive to change. This approach didn't just meet the needs of today's workforce—it set us up for future success. By leading with vulnerability, empathy, grace, authenticity, and humility, I was able to create a work environment where everyone feels valued and empowered to contribute their best.

Incorporating these core values into my leadership style transformed not only my approach but also the entire organization. It created a positive, authentic culture that could navigate challenges and seize opportunities with confidence and integrity. Leading with these values isn't just beneficial—it's essential for any leader who wants to have a lasting effect.

Pivotal Moments Where I Embraced My Core Values to Connect with Others

School Career Fair
Early in my leadership journey, I was asked to speak at a school career fair. Instead of just talking about my achievements, I shared my struggles from school: feeling like an outcast, dealing with self-doubt, and facing academic challenges. This vulnerability struck a chord with the students, bridging the gap between my role as a CEO and their experiences.

The Empathy Workshop
During a leadership retreat, I organized a workshop on empathy and active listening. I shared my own experiences of feeling ignored in school because of a learning disability. This openness created a space

where my team felt comfortable sharing their own vulnerabilities, fostering a culture of understanding and compassion.

The Leadership Seminar
At a leadership seminar, I wove personal stories from my childhood and school years into my talk. Sharing my moments of doubt and how they became opportunities for growth resonated deeply with the audience. Many attendees later shared how my vulnerability inspired them to embrace their own challenges.

The Mentorship Session
In a mentorship session with a young leader, I spoke about my early academic struggles and the mentors who guided me. My vulnerability provided context for my advice, showing that success is built on resilience, learning, and mentorship. The mentee appreciated my candor, finding my path to leadership more relatable and inspiring.

Incorporating your core values into your leadership style isn't just beneficial—it's essential. It makes you a more effective, inspiring, and resilient leader. It builds a positive, authentic culture that can navigate challenges and seize opportunities with confidence and integrity. By leading with your values, you don't just lead—you lead with purpose.

The Power of Vulnerable Leadership
In today's fast-paced, ever-evolving workplace, traditional notions of leadership are being challenged and redefined. Gone are the days when leaders were expected to be infallible, distant, and commanding figures. Modern leadership demands authenticity, empathy, and a willingness to show vulnerability. But why is vulnerable leadership so crucial in today's environment, and how can you, as a leader, embrace and cultivate this quality?

The Case for Vulnerable Leadership

Building Trust and Authentic Connections

At the core of vulnerable leadership is the ability to build genuine trust and connections with your team. When leaders show vulnerability, they humanize themselves, making it easier for team members to relate to them. This authenticity fosters a culture of trust, where employees feel safe to express their ideas, take risks, and share their challenges without fear of judgment or retribution.

Fostering Innovation and Creativity

Innovation thrives in environments where individuals feel safe to experiment, fail, and learn from their mistakes. Vulnerable leaders create such environments by openly sharing their own failures and learning experiences. This openness encourages team members to think creatively, push boundaries, and collaborate more effectively, knowing that their leader supports them regardless of the outcome.

Enhancing Team Morale and Engagement

A leader who demonstrates vulnerability is seen as approachable and empathetic. This approachability boosts team morale and engagement, as employees feel valued and understood. When leaders show that they are not perfect and are willing to seek feedback and input from their team, it empowers employees, making them feel integral to the organization's success.

Driving Personal and Professional Growth

Vulnerable leadership also drives both personal and professional growth. Leaders who embrace vulnerability are more self-aware and open to feedback. This self-awareness allows for continuous personal development and sets an example for their team. By modeling this behavior, leaders encourage their team members to pursue their own growth, fostering a culture of continuous improvement.

How to Become a Vulnerable Leader

Embrace Authenticity

Authenticity is the foundation of vulnerable leadership. Start by being true to yourself and your values. Share your journey, including the challenges and failures you've faced. When your team sees that you are genuine, they are more likely to trust and respect you.

Practice Active Listening

Active listening is a critical component of vulnerable leadership. Make a conscious effort to listen to your team without interrupting or immediately offering solutions. Show empathy and understanding, and validate their feelings and perspectives. This practice not only builds trust but also provides valuable insights into your team's needs and concerns.

Admit Your Mistakes

Admitting your mistakes openly and without defensiveness demonstrates humility and builds credibility. When you own up to your errors and take responsibility, you set a powerful example for your team. It shows that making mistakes is part of the learning process and that it's okay to be imperfect.

Seek Feedback and Act on It

Actively seek feedback from your team and be willing to act on it. This openness to feedback signals that you value their input and are committed to continuous improvement. Create regular opportunities for your team to share their thoughts and suggestions, and show appreciation for their contributions.

Show Empathy and Compassion
Empathy is at the heart of vulnerable leadership. Take the time to understand and connect with your team on a personal level. Show compassion and support when they face challenges, both professionally and personally. By demonstrating that you care about their well-being, you build a loyal and motivated team.

Communicate Transparently
Transparent communication is essential for building trust and fostering a culture of vulnerability. Be open about the organization's goals, challenges, and changes. Share your vision and involve your team in decision-making processes. When your team understands the bigger picture and feels included, they are more likely to be engaged and committed.

Lead by Example
Leading by example is one of the most effective ways to instill vulnerability in your team. Show that you are willing to take risks, admit when you don't have all the answers, and learn from your experiences. Your actions will inspire others to do the same, creating a culture of openness and growth.

In the modern workplace, vulnerable leadership is not just a desirable trait—it's a necessity. By embracing vulnerability, you can build stronger, more authentic relationships with your team, foster innovation, enhance engagement, and drive both personal and professional growth. Remember, being a vulnerable leader doesn't mean being weak; it means being courageous enough to show your true self and create an environment where everyone can thrive. For practical exercises and further guidance on developing vulnerable leadership, refer to the workbook section at the back of this book.

CHAPTER 9

Putting It All Together: Transformative Leadership

> *I have met many entrepreneurs who have the passion and even the work ethic to succeed but who are so obsessed with an idea that they don't see its obvious flaws. Think about that. If you can't even acknowledge your failures, how can you cut the rope and move on?*
> —Kevin O'Leary

Looking back, I can see the successes and failures among the peaks and valleys of my young career as a hospital CEO. Stepping into my new role as CEO, I was brimming with ambition and determined to succeed. Despite my youth and relative inexperience at the executive level, I felt the weight of past doubts. Echoes of being told I'd be "lucky to work at McDonald's" haunted me. Memories of earning just ten dollars an hour as a professional EMT and battling through learning disabilities made self-doubt a constant battle.

But I was not about to let my perceived limitations define me. I embarked on a relentless quest to validate myself as a competent CEO. I seized every learning opportunity, enrolled in relevant courses, devoured self-help books, and soaked up inspiring podcasts. My work ethic was fierce, and my attention to detail was unmatched. No one could tell me I didn't belong at these heights.

However, with this mindset, I found myself going in the wrong direction. In my pursuit of "making it," I lost sight of the immense pressure I was putting on myself. Upon reflection, I realized my intense focus on work came at a significant cost—I had sacrificed precious family time, was working long hours, and placed my career above everything else. It was a painful lesson but one that became a core truth in my life: no job is worth missing out on family time. If I could go back and advise my younger self, I'd stress this lesson. Yet the beauty of life is in its ability to teach through experience. Failures, both professional and personal, have shown me that they are merely stepping-stones to greater success. Every hurdle and every mistake has equipped me with the insight to reach new heights of achievement and fulfillment in every aspect of life. A close friend told me that I was allowing my work to become my identity, which, if you don't know, is extremely unhealthy. I was allowing the organization I was working for dictate who I was, and I began to see my value through the awards and accomplishments I obtained, such as the hospital of excellence awards and Central Penn Business Journal's Forty Under 40 Award. I quickly found my mental health to be poor and my level of happiness nose-dived, even in the middle of much success. I found myself in a moment of needing a perspective change personally and professionally. I needed to get back to my core values and lead through my vulnerability and not by the "successes" on paper or awards.

Transformative Leadership Unveiled

At its heart, transformative leadership challenges the status quo. It empowers people to realize their potential in ways they might never have imagined. Leading with vulnerability isn't a drawback but a superpower that fosters genuine connections and drives meaningful change.

Leadership isn't just a title; it's a force that transcends traditional boundaries and structures, guiding people toward reaching their full potential. Vulnerability gets a bad rap. It's often seen as a crack in the armor, something leaders should avoid. But here's the thing—I've learned that it's actually a superpower. Opening up, showing the real you, is what builds real connections and trust in a team.

Take my own journey as an example. When I first stepped into the role of a young CEO, it felt like I was on a winning streak, lighting up all the dark corners of uncertainty. But even in the midst of these victories, office tensions started to heat up, leading my supervisor and me to agree it was time for a change. My direct supervisor had a completely different vision of leadership and looked at employees as simply that, not human beings. He believed in ruling the roost, where what he wants and says goes, not allowing his employees to have a voice and feel heard. I remember a meeting with him early on in my tenure when he told me that I was allowing my employees too much of a voice and autonomy. He advised me that if this was "going to work," I needed to lead them with authority. I chose to take a stance that day and told him that I was blessed with the opportunity to be a CEO at such a young age because of my approach of vulnerable leadership, leading by example, and leading with empathy and authenticity. I told him that I respected his authority and leadership approach, but I would not waver on my integrity and personal core values in how I lead. This is what began a toxic relationship and led to my decision to move on from the company. This set off a whole new round of thinking about where I wanted my professional life to head next.

Life as a Leader: A Rollercoaster Ride

Life as a leader isn't just about getting to the top; it's about the journey and how you get there. Leadership is like riding a rollercoaster—there are high peaks of success and gut-wrenching drops of setbacks. Leading with vulnerability and your core values can transform both you and your team.

Picture a leader as a beacon of light, cutting through the shadows of criticism and fear. Those leaders who really embrace their vulnerabilities are the ones who spark incredible growth within their organizations. Leadership is a journey of continuous evolution. We see leaders learning the ropes, balancing the grind of work with life at home, and sharing their true selves along the way. They navigate teams full of diverse people, learning to leverage differences as strengths and building trust by showing they're human, too.

Let's explore what makes their leadership tick—how they think, the strategies they use, and the changes they ignite, all while being real and open. What I've definitely learned is that leadership is not a one-size-fits-all journey but a diverse mix of experiences, perspectives, and skills. Leading various teams has taught me invaluable lessons that have shaped not just how I lead but also how I approach team development. Here they are:

Embrace the Chaos
Leadership isn't always about having everything under control. Sometimes, it's about managing the chaos and guiding your team through it. Don't freak out when things get messy; instead, use those moments to show your team that you can handle pressure and adapt.

Listen More Than You Speak
You've got two ears and one mouth for a reason. Great leaders listen to their team members. It's not just about hearing their words but understanding their concerns, ideas, and feedback. Make it a point to genuinely listen and watch how your team feels more valued and engaged.

Lead by Example
Your actions speak louder than words. If you want your team to be punctual, dedicated, and hardworking, you better be the first one in and the last one out. Show them the standards you expect through your own behavior.

Foster a Culture of Trust
Trust is the foundation of any successful team. Be transparent with your team, admit your mistakes, and show them that you trust them to do their jobs. When your team knows you have their back, they'll have yours.

Encourage Personal Growth
Your team's development should be a priority. Encourage them to pursue their passions, offer opportunities for learning, and support their career aspirations. When individuals grow, so does the team.

Celebrate Small Wins
Big achievements are great, but don't overlook the small victories. Celebrating small wins boosts morale and keeps the team motivated. A little recognition goes a long way.

Don't Micromanage
Nobody likes a boss who's always looking over their shoulder. Trust your team to do their jobs and give them the space to do it. Micromanagement stifles creativity and kills motivation.

Be Human
Show your team that you're not just a boss but a human being. Share your own struggles, be approachable, and show empathy. When your

team sees your human side, they're more likely to connect with you and be inspired by your leadership.

Adaptability is Key
Things rarely go as planned. The best leaders are those who can pivot and adapt to new situations. Show your team that flexibility is a strength and that being open to change can lead to better outcomes.

Have Fun
Work doesn't have to be all serious all the time. Create an environment where your team can have fun, be themselves, and enjoy coming to work. A happy team is a productive team.

Leading diverse teams and promoting growth requires humility, empathy, and a commitment to continuous improvement. By embracing diversity, fostering inclusion, building trust, empowering through mentorship, and cultivating a learning environment, I've not only enhanced my leadership but also witnessed the profound growth of individuals who might have remained under the radar. Through it all, I've seen that when diverse minds collaborate toward a common goal, incredible progress isn't just possible—it's inevitable.

Leading with vulnerability has transformed not only my leadership style but also the culture of the teams I've been a part of. It's about being real, showing empathy, and creating an environment where everyone can thrive. As we look to the future, these qualities will be more important than ever in navigating the complexities of our ever-changing world.

Seizing Opportunities in Greenville, South Carolina

After I learned my lesson from the peaks and valleys we talked about in my early tenure as a hospital CEO, I took on a role at a brand-new hospital in Greenville, South Carolina. It was a perfect match for my leadership style and ambitions. So, just like that, my family and I were off to Greenville, ready to help shape the future of a hospital that was still just blueprints and building blocks. Starting fresh allowed me to build a team from the ground up and really embed my vision into our culture from day one. As the big opening day approached, we all gathered to bless this new beginning. Greenville wasn't just a new home; it became the place where I truly found my groove as a leader, leaning into vulnerability and empowering my team. The effort and dedication paid off, and I was honored to be named the CEO of the Year by the Greenville Business Journal. This recognition wasn't just a personal achievement; it was a testament to the power of leading with my core values.

Core Values and Vulnerable Leadership

My personal core values have been my anchor through all of this. Values such as vulnerability, empathy, and a relentless pursuit of growth have guided me, even when the path was unclear. These values helped me stay true to myself, and they made me realize the power of vulnerable and transformative leadership.

Seeing the positive effects of this approach was like a lightbulb moment for me. It wasn't just about achieving business goals; it was about making a meaningful difference in people's lives. That's what inspired me to share the power of transformative leadership with others. I wanted to show that true leadership is about lifting others up, creating a supportive environment, and driving collective success.

CHAPTER 10

Passing On the Torch

Go into all the world and proclaim the gospel to the whole creation.
—Jesus Christ

Reflecting on my journey, I realize how each chapter has shaped who I am today. It's been a wild mix of lessons learned, challenges smashed, and wins celebrated. But this chapter? It's not just about me. It's about the legacy I leave and the path I pave for those who will walk it after me.

I've been lucky to have mentors who had my back when I doubted myself. They were my lifeline through some pretty rough seas. Now, standing at the threshold of what's next, I see how crucial it is for me to light the way for others.

Passing on the torch isn't about bragging about my successes; it's about showing the real, gritty journey through the mess-ups, doubts, and tough times. It's about showing that true greatness comes through grinding it out when things get tough and building a community that finds strength in being real and sees opportunities in every setback.

True leadership, to me, is about rolling with your flaws and leading with your heart, not just putting on a slick show. It's about sharing our real stories—the times we stumbled, the times we doubted, and the times we pushed through anyway. These stories connect us, bridging the gap between us and those looking up to us.

Becoming Better Leaders Through Vulnerability, Core Values, and Transformative Leadership

Vulnerable Leadership

Vulnerable leadership is all about being authentic, transparent, and empathetic with your team. It's about showing that you're human, too, and that you don't have all the answers. Here are some tips on becoming a better leader through vulnerable leadership:

Share Your Struggles: Talk openly about the challenges you've faced and how you overcame them. This not only humanizes you but also encourages others to share their experiences.

Ask for Help: Demonstrating that you don't have all the answers can foster a collaborative environment where everyone feels valued and empowered to contribute.

Show Empathy: Understanding and addressing the emotional needs of your team can build trust and loyalty. Be genuinely interested in their well-being and challenges.

Live Your Core Values

Your core values are the foundation of your leadership. They guide your decisions, actions, and interactions. To lead effectively, you must consistently align your behavior with these values:

Define Your Values: Clearly articulate what matters most to you. Whether it's integrity, innovation, or compassion, make sure these values are at the forefront of your leadership.

Model Your Values: Lead by example. Demonstrate your commitment to your values through your actions, and your team will follow suit.

Communicate Your Values: Regularly discuss your values with your team. Highlight how these values shape your goals and decisions, reinforcing their importance.

Practice Transformative Leadership

Transformative leadership goes beyond managing tasks and projects; it's about inspiring and motivating others to achieve their full potential. Here's how to cultivate transformative leadership:

Empower Others: Encourage your team to take ownership of their work and provide them with the resources and support they need to succeed. Trust them to make decisions and innovate.

Create a Vision: Paint a compelling picture of the future that excites and motivates your team. Make sure everyone understands their role in achieving this vision.

Foster a Growth Mindset: Encourage continuous learning and development. Provide opportunities for your team to expand their skills and knowledge, and celebrate their progress.

Helpful Insights

If I could give one piece of advice, it would be to really embrace the journey of growing, both personally and professionally. Here's a deeper dive into that:

Define Your Purpose: Know what drives you. What fires you up? Your purpose is your guiding star. Really think about what matters to you and let that guide your growth.

Build Resilience: Growth often comes with its set of challenges. View setbacks as opportunities to learn and get stronger. Remember, it's not about how often you fall; it's about how often you bounce back.

Keep Learning: The world's changing fast. Stay sharp by embracing lifelong learning—read up, take courses, find mentors, and hit those workshops.

Embrace Change: Change is inevitable. Instead of fearing it, see it as a chance to discover new strengths and opportunities.

Build Your Tribe: Surround yourself with folks who lift you up. Find mentors, friends, and colleagues who support you and can be your safety net when things get tough.

Take Smart Risks: To grow, sometimes you need to step out of your comfort zone. Take calculated risks that could lead to major breakthroughs.

Be Kind to Yourself: You'll mess up sometimes—treat yourself with kindness and remember that every mistake is a step toward greater things.

Stay Flexible: Being adaptable is a superpower in today's world. Use change and uncertainty as chances to try new paths and solutions.

Set Goals and Celebrate: Have clear goals and take time to celebrate when you hit them. Recognizing your wins, big or small, fuels your drive to keep pushing.

Give Back: As you grow, don't forget to lift others up. Sharing your knowledge through mentorship not only helps others but also enriches your own journey.

Be an Inspiration

Looking back from my early days to becoming a CEO, I'm grateful for every twist and turn. Here's the real talk on what I've learned about being true to yourself and leading effectively:

Embrace Genuine Leadership: Staying true to who you are and your vision, even when it goes against the grain, is crucial. It wasn't easy, but it was always right.

Challenge Conformity: Early on, I felt pressure to just agree and not rock the boat. But to create an environment where people felt valued, I had to stand firm in my beliefs.

Value Your People: You can't do it alone. Celebrate your team's hard work and dedication—they're your biggest asset.

Recognize Your Worth: Don't tie your worth just to your job title or achievements. You're valuable because of your unique traits and the positive effect you can have.

Lead by Example: Show what it means to be resilient and committed. Your actions inspire those around you.

Celebrate Milestones: Celebrate every achievement. It's a reminder that with persistence, anything is possible.

Manage Stress: Leadership is tough. I've battled anxiety, which taught me the importance of self-care and seeking help when needed.

Lighting the Path for Others

Passing the torch is about lighting the way for future leaders to be their best selves, grounded in their values, and ready to make a difference. Embrace your journey, lead with intention, and inspire those around you to do the same. The path to leadership is as much about affecting others as it is about achieving your own goals.

How to Pass on the Torch
Identify Your Personal Core Values

First things first, you've got to know what you stand for. Your personal core values are your guiding principles. They're the non-negotiables that shape your decisions and actions. Here's how to get started:

Reflect on Your Experiences: Look back at the pivotal moments in your life. What values were at play when you felt most fulfilled or challenged? Write these down.

Seek Feedback: Ask those who know you well to describe the values they see you living by. Sometimes, an outside perspective can be incredibly insightful.

Prioritize Your Values: List out your core values and rank them. Which ones are absolutely essential? Which ones guide you in tough times?

Lead with Vulnerability

Leading with vulnerability means showing up as your authentic self, warts and all. It's about being real with your team and creating an environment where they feel safe to do the same. Here's how to lead with vulnerability:

Share Your Story: Let your team in on your journey—the highs, the lows, and the lessons learned. This transparency builds trust and shows that it's okay to be human.

Admit Your Mistakes: When you mess up, own it. Apologize and explain what you've learned. This sets a powerful example of accountability and growth.

Ask for Help: Show that you don't have all the answers by seeking input from your team. This not only empowers them but also fosters a collaborative environment.

Transformative Leadership

Transformative leadership is about inspiring and motivating your team to exceed their own expectations. It's about creating a vision that others want to be a part of. Here's how to practice transformative leadership:

Create a Compelling Vision: Paint a vivid picture of what success looks like. Your vision should be inspiring and align with your core values.

Empower Your Team: Give your team the tools, resources, and autonomy they need to succeed. Trust them to take ownership of their work.

Celebrate Successes: Recognize and celebrate both individual and team achievements. This reinforces positive behavior and keeps everyone motivated.

Lighting the Path for Others

Now, let's dive into the art of passing the torch. I'm talking about how to be that spark for the next generation.

Mentor with Intention: Take the time to mentor emerging leaders. Share your insights, provide guidance, and be a sounding board for their ideas and challenges.

Encourage Self-Discovery: Help future leaders identify their own core values. Encourage them to reflect, seek feedback, and prioritize what matters most to them.

Model Vulnerability: Show them what it looks like to lead with vulnerability. Be open about your journey and the lessons you've learned along the way.

Foster a Culture of Growth: Create an environment where continuous learning and development are prioritized. Provide opportunities for your team to grow and evolve.

Inspire with Your Vision: Share your vision and encourage others to develop their own. Help them see how they can contribute to something bigger than themselves.

As my own guides have done for me, I'm here to light the path for others. This book is about inspiring and empowering those around me—not just celebrating my own wins. I'm driven by a mission to create waves of resilience, inspiration, and growth that reach way beyond my own steps.

Passing the torch is about more than just handing off responsibilities; it's about igniting a passion for leadership in others. It's about ensuring that the values and lessons you hold dear continue to live on through the leaders you inspire. So, embrace your journey, lead with intention, and inspire those around you to do the same. The path to leadership is as much about affecting others as it is about achieving your own goals.

Conclusion

Dear Reader,

Faith has been an unshakable anchor throughout my life. It has been the guiding light that has enabled me to face hardship head on, learn from my mistakes, and break free from the crushing grasp of self-doubt. Although the scars of the past will never completely heal, I've learned how to transform them into sources of power. These experiences have given me a unique capacity to counsel and encourage people based on my challenges and accomplishments. Whatever problems lay ahead, I've learned to persist with unyielding tenacity. To genuinely understand the importance within, we must sometimes peel back the layers and accept vulnerability. Our individual and communal importance begins to emerge as a result of this openness.

As I consider my life's purpose, I realize that leaving a lasting legacy and positively influencing others is the most important; these are the pursuits that bring genuine fulfillment, far exceeding any superficial measures of success. Through faith, resilience, and a commitment to making a difference, we can all leave our mark on this world, no matter where we come from or where we're going.

- **Resilience:** We've all been through things that might have broken us, but here we are. I learned the power of resilience along the way. It's not so much about being impenetrable as it is about finding the fortitude to repair, adapt, and emerge even stronger.
- **Leadership:** Leadership is a calling, not a title. My journey took me from self-doubt to the CEO's chair, but titles never

defined my value. What counts most is the legacy we leave behind, the people we affect, and the positive change we inspire. Leadership does not include being a "yes man," but rather having the guts to stick to your principles and vision in the face of adversity.

- **Personal Growth:** Our history does not determine our future; rather, it prepares us for it. Every obstacle and every setback is a chance for progress. I've discovered that self-worth isn't dependent on professional achievement or external affirmation. It's about accepting your shortcomings, receiving help when necessary, and realizing that your mistakes are stepping-stones to greatness.

Now is the time for you to act. Accept the concept of vulnerable leadership. It is about leading authentically, using your experiences and mistakes to mold your leadership style. It's about transforming failure into a source of growth and strength.

Keep in mind that you are not alone. It's acceptable to not be okay all of the time. It is okay to ask for assistance, to be vulnerable, and to lead with your heart. You not only improve your own life by doing so but also build a culture of honesty and progress for those you lead.

In the end, it is not our titles, honors, or financial achievements that define us. It is the difference we make, the lessons we teach, and the legacy we leave behind. Your path may have been different from mine, but we all can change our lives and inspire others.

So face your future with confidence, embrace the leader who resides within you, and strive to be the best version of yourself. Like mine, your path has the potential to be spectacular.

With unshakable faith in your potential,

Joshua P. Trout, MHA

Study Workbook

Objective: This workbook will help you identify and cultivate your core values, guiding your leadership journey and influencing those around you. You will reflect on your experiences, define your values, and create a plan to live them out in your leadership role.

Reference Chapter: Chapter 7: The Compass of Transformative Leadership and Cultivating Your Core Values

Exercise 1: Reflecting on Past Experiences
Recall Proud Moments:
1. Think about three moments in your life when you felt the most proud. Write them down and explain why these moments stood out to you.
2. What values were you upholding during these moments?

Identify Painful Experiences:
1. Reflect on three challenging or painful experiences you've had. Describe them in detail.
2. What values were violated in these situations? What did you learn about yourself and your values?

Exercise 2: Admiring Influences
List Influential Figures:
1. Identify three people you admire (they could be mentors, family members, historical figures, etc.).
2. What values do these individuals embody that you find inspiring?

Connect to Your Values:
1. Compare the qualities you admire in others to your own experiences. What values do you share with these influential figures?
2. How can these values guide your leadership style?

Exercise 3: Identifying Core Values

List Potential Core Values:
1. Create a list of potential core values (e.g., integrity, compassion, innovation, respect, transparency).
2. Highlight the values that resonate most with you.

Narrow Down Your Core Values:
1. Select your top five to seven core values from the list.
2. Write a brief definition of each value in your own words.

Exercise 4: Living Your Values

Daily Rituals:
1. Develop a daily ritual to practice one of your core values. For example, if compassion is a core value, start each day by checking in on a team member.
2. Describe the ritual and how it aligns with your core values.

Weekly Reflection:
1. Set aside time each week to reflect on your actions and decisions. Did they align with your core values?
2. Write about a situation in which you upheld your values and a situation in which you struggled. What can you learn from these experiences?

Exercise 5: Values in Action
Scenario Analysis:
1. Think about a recent challenging situation at work. Describe the situation and how you handled it.
2. Reflect on whether your actions aligned with your core values. If not, how could you handle a similar situation differently in the future?

Team Engagement:
1. Share your core values with your team. Explain why these values are important to you and how they will guide your leadership.
2. Ask your team to share their core values. How can you support them in living out their values at work?

Objective: This workbook will help you identify and cultivate vulnerable leadership practices, guiding your leadership journey and influencing those around you. You will reflect on your experiences, define your approach, and create a plan to live out vulnerability in your leadership role.

Reference Chapter: Chapter 8: My Personal Core Values: Embracing Vulnerability, Empathy, Grace, Authenticity, and Humility

Exercise 1: Reflecting on Authentic Leadership
Recall Proud Moments:
1. Think about three moments in your life when you felt the most proud. Write them down and explain why these moments stood out to you.
2. What values were you upholding during these moments?

Identify Painful Experiences:
1. Reflect on three challenging or painful experiences you've had. Describe them in detail.
2. What values were violated in these situations? What did you learn about yourself and your values?

Exercise 4: Living Vulnerability
Daily Rituals:
1. Develop a daily ritual to practice one of your core values. For example, if compassion is a core value, start each day by checking in on a team member.
2. Describe the ritual and how it aligns with your core values.

Weekly Reflection:
1. Set aside time each week to reflect on your actions and decisions. Did they align with your core values?
2. Write about a situation in which you upheld your values and a situation in which you struggled. What can you learn from these experiences?

Exercise 5: Vulnerability in Action
Scenario Analysis:
1. Think about a recent challenging situation at work. Describe the situation and how you handled it.
2. Reflect on whether your actions aligned with your core values. If not, how could you handle a similar situation differently in the future?

Team Engagement:
1. Share your core values with your team. Explain why these values are important to you and how they will guide your leadership.
2. Ask your team to share their core values. How can you support them in living out their values at work?

Conclusion
Reflect on your journey through this workbook. What key insights have you gained about vulnerable leadership? How will you continue to develop this important trait?

Use this workbook regularly to assess and refine your approach to vulnerable leadership. Remember, vulnerability is a strength that can transform your leadership and your team's success.

Objective: This part of the workbook will help you integrate the principles of transformative and vulnerable leadership into your daily practice. You will create a comprehensive leadership development plan and reflect on your growth.

Reference Chapter: Chapter 9: Putting It All Together: Transformative Leadership

Exercise 1: Comprehensive Leadership Development Plan

Integrate Your Learnings:
1. Reflect on the exercises from Chapters 7 and 8; How have these practices shaped your understanding of transformative and vulnerable leadership?
2. Write a summary of the key insights and lessons you have learned.

Develop Your Plan:
1. Create a detailed leadership development plan. Include your vision, core values, goals, strategies for fostering innovation, and methods for navigating change.
2. Identify specific actions you will take to live out your values and inspire your team.

Exercise 2: Reflecting on Your Journey

Personal Reflection:
1. Reflect on your journey as a leader. What challenges have you overcome, and what successes have you achieved?
2. Write about how your leadership style has evolved and the effect it has had on your team and organization.

Feedback and Growth:
1. Seek feedback from your team and peers. What do they appreciate about your leadership, and where do they see opportunities for growth?
2. Use this feedback to identify areas for continuous improvement and set new goals for your leadership development.

Exercise 3: Celebrating Milestones and Achievements
Track Your Progress:
1. Review your leadership development plan regularly. Track your progress toward your goals, and celebrate your achievements.
2. Write about a recent milestone you have reached and the steps you took to get there.

Recognize Your Team:
1. Identify and celebrate the contributions of your team members. How have they supported your vision and goals?
2. Plan a recognition event or activity to show your appreciation for their hard work and dedication.

This workbook is designed to be a practical guide for you as you embark on your leadership journey. By reflecting on your experiences, identifying and living by your core values, and implementing transformative and vulnerable leadership practices, you will inspire and empower those around you, creating a lasting effect.

Acknowledgements

I would like to express my heartfelt gratitude to those who have significantly contributed to my journey and success.

First and foremost, I want to acknowledge the late Lorraine Quinter, the school secretary at my elementary school. Lorraine's unwavering dedication to my education and well-being ensured that I always had the best teachers to meet my learning disabilities and personal needs. Her kindness and support have left an indelible mark on my life, and I am forever grateful for her efforts.

I owe a tremendous debt of gratitude to Bonnie England. Bonnie provided me with invaluable assistance during my struggles with math and self-confidence. Her innovative and engaging teaching methods, including the creation of educational games, played a crucial role in helping me grasp mathematical concepts quickly and effectively. Bonnie's belief in me and her commitment to my development had the most significant effect on my journey as a student facing challenges. I credit her with guiding me through the most difficult times in my education and fostering the confidence I needed to succeed.

I also want to thank Joann Marn for her dedication and support outside of school as my tutor. Joann helped me immensely with learning how to read, and her favorite saying, "Don't put the caboose before the engine," resonated with me as I often tried to read too quickly to reach the end of a sentence. Her guidance and patience were instrumental in improving my reading skills and building my confidence.

A special thank you to Melanie Castellana, the mother of my friend Joey. Melanie, who also worked at the school, watched over me and provided unwavering support. Her continued encouragement and belief in me have made a world of difference. Melanie remains one of my biggest supporters to this day, and her support means the world to me.

I extend my deepest appreciation to Paula Suchko, my Easterseals speech therapist. Paula played a huge role in teaching me how to speak during my early childhood years as I worked through chronic illnesses and ear problems. Her dedication and expertise were crucial in helping me develop my speech skills and preparing me to enter elementary school. I owe a lot to her for getting me speaking and setting a strong foundation for my education.

I also want to recognize and thank all the special needs teachers throughout my educational years. They played a significant role in getting me through school, providing the support and guidance I needed to overcome my challenges. Their patience, understanding, and commitment have been invaluable to my success.

A big shoutout to Scott Deutsch, a friend and the fire chief of Jefferson Hills Fire/Rescue, where I worked as a firefighter. Scott was someone I looked up to and always sought to learn from. He was part of a pivotal moment in my life when we were enjoying coffee at the firehouse together. I was having a pity party about my life, feeling like I was never going to advance in my career since I had no higher education. Scott gave me tough love and told me to stop feeling sorry for myself and to do something with my life. He encouraged me to go to school and make it happen. I took that tough love and ran with it. I owe him a big shoutout for kicking me in the butt and pushing me to pursue my education and career goals.

Another pivotal moment in my career was when I worked at a hospice agency and had a follow-up meeting with my new manager, Barbara. She told me that I was a great hospice representative and that she could tell by my interactions with her that I wanted to be a leader someday. She said I would be a great leader but would never be successful as one because I was "too black and white." I was initially annoyed with this comment but quickly did self-reflection and realized that she was absolutely correct. If it wasn't for her tough love, I am not sure I would have corrected this bad habit. Barbara's insight and honesty helped me grow immensely, and I am deeply grateful for her guidance.

I want to thank Patrick Tuer, who was my regional vice president while I was a business development director. Pat was someone I looked up to, and I wanted to follow in his footsteps. Pat saw something in me that I didn't see in myself. He consistently gave me opportunities to show the company what I was capable of. Pat was the one who approached me about being a CEO of a hospital and motivated me to apply. He saw something in me and believed in me, and I cannot ever put into words how much that meant to me. If not for his pushing me and motivating me, I am not sure my career path would have gone the way that it has. I am blessed to still call him a friend and work in the same organization as him. I love celebrating his successes and will forever be indebted to him.

I want to thank my fire and EMS family for always being supportive of my dreams, specifically my good friends Mike Dziki and Matt Smelser. Matt's story was provided in the book, and I owe so much to him; he will be forever missed. Mike is still a close friend, and I thank him for always listening to me vent about my dreams and aspirations while we worked our twenty-four-hour shifts together. Their support and camaraderie have been invaluable to me.

I want to thank my entire family for their love and support throughout this journey and for showing me what it is to have an entrepreneurial spirit and hard work ethic. This goes from my aunt owning her own business, to my nephew's unwavering faith, and to my sister and parents for their work ethic and use of their God-given gifts. I would like to give a special mention to my Uncle George, who was a professional artist for a large organization for many years. He was one of the few examples I had in my life at that time who had a degree, put it to use, and was successful. I loved going to his work as a child and seeing him in his environment. It gave me the desire to make something of myself, get a degree, and be a professional someday just like him. My father was another great example for me that it's never too late to go back to school, make a change, and better your life by doing something you love.

Lastly, I want to thank my wife, Julie, and daughter, Hannah, for supporting me during the long hours working twenty-four-hour shifts multiple times a week and coming home, spending minimal time with them before locking myself in the office and doing school for many years. I can't thank my wife enough for pushing me to go back to school and chase my dreams to better our lives as a family. Without her push and support, I would not be here today. I also thank my wife and daughter for their sacrifices during this time and for their willingness to move multiple times for the next best step for my career. I could not have done this without them!

Thank you, Lorraine, Bonnie, Joann, Melanie, Paula, Scott, Barbara, Pat, Mike, Matt, Uncle George, my parents, Julie, Hannah, and all the special needs teachers, for your profound influence on my life. Your contributions have been instrumental in shaping who I am today.

In Loving Memory

Honoring Matt: The Brotherhood That Never Dies

Matt was one of my first EMS mentors. He was a man of integrity, strength, and fairness. Always dressed impeccably, he exuded professionalism in everything he did. Matt was someone you could rely on, who knew his stuff inside and out. He had a profound effect on me. Looking back, I realize how much I looked up to him during my early years in EMS. His influence was unforgettable.

Matt played a huge role in shaping my outlook on leadership. His authenticity and commitment to his core values were a game changer for me. He showed me that being a great leader isn't just about making the right decisions; it's about staying true to your values and being genuine. Even now, I pay attention to my appearance—not to be on a magazine cover but to show integrity, confidence, and genuine care for my work. I owe that to Matt, who was a living example of what it takes to be a great leader.

Love you, brother!